WORLD WAR II BIOGRAPHIES

MUSSOLINI
AND ITALIAN FASCISM

M · MULVIHILL

FRANKLIN WATTS

London · New York · Toronto · Sydney

THE EARLY YEARS

Benito Mussolini was born on 29 July 1883 in the village of Predappio, near Forli, in the Romagna, a rugged, hilly region in northern Italy which was famous for its revolutionary political culture. His father was a blacksmith and his mother a schoolteacher.

Mussolini as an ardent young revolutionary in Switzerland, 1904. Although these years away from Italy were full of hardship, they were also the years of Mussolini's political apprenticeship. He never forgot the importance of propaganda, and the usefulness of violence.

The family lived in a small cottage attached to the school and although they were poor, they had some social standing in their village. As well as his mother's status as the local teacher, Mussolini's father was respected as an active and fearless socialist. Alessandro Mussolini's politics were evident in the naming of his eldest son "Benito" in honour of Benito Juarez, the Mexican revolutionary leader.

However, Mussolini's mother was more traditional in her beliefs and expectations. A devout Catholic, she insisted that her sons had a full education – unusual for peasant boys from the Romagna – and even hoped for a time that Benito might become a priest. But from his earliest days it was obvious that in personality Benito Mussolini was most like his unruly, fiercely anti-clerical father. His childhood friends remembered him as a bully and a *teppista* (hooligan), and he was expelled from one secondary school after he stabbed another boy. Right from the beginning Mussolini had no qualms about resorting to violence.

In spite of his delinquency, Mussolini was clever enough to persist with his schooling and he qualified as a primary schoolteacher in 1902. By then he had intellectual ambitions, reading voraciously and writing poems and novels. Yet even though Mussolini continued his education, eventually taking an examination in French which qualified him to teach in secondary schools, he did not settle into teaching. In every teaching job he quickly ran into trouble with parents because of the bad example he set the children as a gambler, a heavy drinker and a womaniser.

When his first teaching job ended, in June 1902, he left Italy for Switzerland, where many Italians emigrated to work. It is probable that he left Italy to avoid military service. However, it is also plausible that other factors – debts, awkward love affairs and a desire to see more of the world – also played a part in his move. When Mussolini became dictator of Italy, great care was taken to cleanse his early life story of any incidents that were not consistent with his fascist image: for example, his hostility to the church, and his earlier socialist convictions.

The young Mussolini spent the two most miserable years of his life working in Switzerland at all sorts of menial jobs, including labouring and working for a wine-seller and a butcher. But among the poor and illiterate Italian workers in Switzerland, Mussolini, with his superior education and radical background, soon emerged as a revolutionary agitator. As such he was expelled from Switzerland, the police report describing him as an "impulsive and violent" young man. On his return to Italy he performed his military service.

Once back in his native Romagna, he became a leading member of the local socialist movement. At the end of 1908 he went to Trento to work on a socialist newspaper. Because this city was then part of Austria-Hungary (the empire in Central Europe), Mussolini became an ardent "Irredentist" – that is, he believed that Italy's frontiers should be changed to include all ethnic Italians. For the Irredentists, Italy's "natural" frontiers included not only the areas around the cities of Trento and Trieste, but also most of Dalmatia (present-day Yugoslavia). Patriots believed force should be used if necessary to wrest the territories from Austria-Hungary.

Mussolini's mother had died in February 1905, which meant that his father had to leave the family cottage (which was owned by the school) to make way for a new schoolteacher. By now Alessandro Mussolini was living with another woman and Benito Mussolini married her daughter, Rachele. Rachele Mussolini was a sensible, unpretentious peasant woman whose chief concern in life was the upbringing of the five children she had by Mussolini, who nearly always had another woman in his life. Their first and favourite child, Edda, was born in 1910. But life with Mussolini would never be calm. He was frequently in trouble with the authorities for his subversive activities, and in 1911 he was imprisoned for protesting against Italy's colonial war in Libya. Along with many other socialists, Mussolini condemned this war of imperialism as an attempt by the government to distract the country from domestic problems such as unemployment.

A year after his trial and imprisonment, which made him famous beyond the Romagna, he became editor of the Socialist Party's daily news-paper, *Avanti!* (*Forward!*), which was based in Milan. His fiery speeches and punchy articles earned him more celebrity in the years leading up to World War I. Throughout his career Mussolini used his newspaper experience, always thinking of catchy slogans and strong headlines.

When World War I broke out in 1914 Mussolini was, like many socialists, in favour of absolute neutrality for Italy. But then he changed his mind, believing that if Italy sided with France and Britain against Germany and Austria-Hungary, the nation might be rewarded after victory with extra territory. He also believed that in the upheaval workers would have opportunities to seize political power. He then broke with the Socialist Party and set up his own newspaper, *Il Popolo d'Italia* (*The People of Italy*). In a few years this would become the official paper of the fascist movement. In August 1915 he was called up to serve in the army, spending the next 17 months as a soldier until, after being wounded in February 1917, he resumed work with his newspaper.

After World War I there was great disappointment in Italy because the Treaty of Versailles did not give the country the territories it thought were

Mussolini as a soldier in the Italian Army. Although at first he claimed to be a pacifist, he was a willing fighter. Early in 1917, during a training exercise, a grenade thrower he was using exploded, killing several people and leaving him with 40 fragments in his body. Although this wound was not serious, Mussolini glorified the incident as a moment of extreme personal bravery.

its due. Italy had after all joined the winning side: that of Britain, France, Russia and the United States. The post-war settlement, however, gave Dalmatia to the newly independent nation of Yugoslavia. Italian Irredentists were outraged. In September 1919 the poet Gabriele D'Annunzio led a raid on the port of Fiume on the Adriatic coast, by then Yugoslavian territory, supported by mutinous elements of the Italian Army. Mussolini was by that time associated with the leadership of a group of extremely nationalistic anti-socialist ex-soldiers. He had previously discussed the possibility of such a raid, and was annoyed at first that the poet had upstaged him. Now, however, he tried to claim some of the credit for D'Annunzio's success and it was from the flamboyant poet that he borrowed many of the rituals of the fascist movement. To keep D'Annunzio satisfied Mussolini later made him into a prince and had all his works lavishly published.

In that same year, with financial aid from industrialists and big landowners who were fearful of a revolution in Italy, Mussolini organised his followers into a militia called *Fasci di Combattimento*. The word *fascio* comes from the Latin *fascis*, which literally means "a bundle" and refers to the bundle of sticks, symbolising justice, carried by Roman officials in processions during the Roman Empire. Because of its associations with the solemn rites of Italy's imperial past, *fascio* was not an unusual name for Italian radical groups.

Mussolini's fascists wore black shirts, just as the followers of Garibaldi, the great leader of the *Risorgimento*, the Italian unification movement of the 19th century, had worn red shirts. The Black Shirts adopted a distinctive salute, outstretching their arms, and their special weapon was a bludgeon called the *manganello*. These men, who were notorious for forcing their opponents to drink castor oil, lived up to their motto *"me ne frego"* ("I don't give a damn") and Mussolini was *il Duce* (the leader). As far as possible, the *Duce*'s personal involvement with their crimes was kept secret, but he knew what his followers were doing and was responsible for them. Only he could control the Black Shirts.

The fascists had contradictory aims. Mussolini made up his policy as he went along, borrowing from socialist theory, German philosophy, French syndicalism (a theory that trade unions are the basis for transforming society), even Catholic theology, as it suited him. Apart from its strong anti-socialist origins, the only consistent thing about fascist ideology was its emphasis on action and on the necessity of physical force to bring about political change. Fascism celebrated war for its own sake. It was born of a "need for action and in itself was action".

Mussolini was an expert and commanding public speaker. With his enormous square head, his jutting jaw, his stern eyes and his barking voice, he radiated brute strength. Apart from those people who saw Mussolini's fascists as the best way to fight the rise of socialism, there were many who were simply longing for a strong government to take control of a chaotic, strike-ridden Italy. By 1920, when he was 37, Mussolini's movement had gained a foothold in parliament.

THE MARCH ON ROME

In November 1921, Mussolini's movement, by now a well-organised political party, announced its programme: social reform, national prestige abroad, restoration of law and order, financial stability, and above all, a strong state. There were 2,300 local fascist groups and these claimed some 320,000 members.

Flaunting pictures of Marx and Lenin which were probably taken from ransacked socialist buildings, Mussolini's Black Shirts arrive in Rome. Later, those fascists who participated in the stage-managed March on Rome were honoured as pioneering heroes of the movement.

The weak coalition government which came to power in 1922 was quite unable to deal with the unrest in Italy and as the prospect of civil war loomed, Mussolini prepared to take power. In August of that year his fascists broke a general strike by organising essential services themselves. As part of this operation they became practised in seizing control of railway stations and telephone exchanges, as well as destroying trade union buildings and socialist newspaper offices. In October this experience was used to mount a very elaborate operation, by which the fascists occupied all the lines of communication between the north of Italy and the capital of Rome.

Meanwhile Mussolini remained in Milan, awaiting a call from King Victor Emmanuel III. Fearful of civil war, or worse, a socialist revolution that would abolish the monarchy, Victor Emmanuel thought that Mussolini offered the best hope of survival for his dynasty. Mussolini knew this. His willingness to compromise, so long as his movement gained power, showed itself in his relations with the king. Until then Mussolini had been, in theory, against monarchy and in favour of a republican constitution for Italy. But when the king showed himself to be a willing tool for the rise of fascism, Mussolini let it be known that he would be happy to accommodate Victor Emmanuel as a figurehead monarch of Italy. By keeping the goodwill of the king, he also reassured his right-wing, royalist supporters. It was not long before the royal summons came, an invitation to become the country's premier. Mussolini set off for Rome by train, arriving in triumph on 30 October. This

was the so-called "March on Rome", which was stage-managed as a triumphal entry into the capital city.

Although Mussolini soon established himself as a dictator, he began his rule as the head of a coalition government with the co-operation of several democratic groups. It was a year later, in 1923, when he began to introduce the changes in the electoral system that would ensure total control by the fascists. By the Acerbo Law, the political party which came top of the poll, provided it had 25 per cent of the votes, was entitled to two-thirds of the seats in parliament, the remainder being divided proportionally among the other political parties. In the elections of April 1924 the fascists, in alliance with nationalists, did secure 65.25 per

Knowing that the way is clear for him to seize political power, the *Duce* himself arrives in Rome, to be greeted by his jubilant henchmen. Whatever the shabby realities, good photo-opportunities were essential to Mussolini's triumph. The scale of the fascist March on Rome was much smaller than propaganda claimed, but no one called the *Duce*'s bluff.

cent of the votes and therefore an overwhelming majority of seats. However, this electoral victory was achieved in an atmosphere of fascist terror. One socialist candidate was murdered, while others were beaten up. The voting itself was also interfered with: dead people's names were added to the electoral roll, opposition voting papers were destroyed and in some areas more than 100 per cent of the registered electorate voted! When the socialist leader, Giacomo Matteotti, protested in parliament and asked for the election result to be declared invalid, Mussolini had no scruples about encouraging his followers to deal with him in their usual way. Giacomo Matteotti was murdered.

After this outrage, opposition deputies united in an attempt to oust Mussolini from power, but the *Duce* kept his nerve. On 3 January 1925 he declared that in future no opposition to his rule would be tolerated. From this time on, he made no pretence of running a democratic government. Within a few months what survived of the anti-fascist press was banned and dissolved, all secret societies were forbidden and only the new fascist trade unions had the right to negotiate with employers. The persecution of anti-fascists, always an activity of the Black Shirt squads, now became official government policy. To preserve "social hygiene", political prisoners were detained in penal settlements established on Lipari and other islands. A lighter punishment was detention in some specified village in a remote area of south Italy. Anyone sent to *confino* (prison) was not allowed to appeal against the decision, and of course it was all done in the strictest secrecy.

Antonio Gramsci, the intellectual leader of the small Italian Communist Party, died in 1937 after 11 years as a political prisoner.

Mussolini summed up fascist policy as "Everything for the State, nothing against the State, nothing outside the State". By the end of 1925 Mussolini was the head of government, responsible only to the powerless king, as opposed to a cabinet of ministers and a chamber of parliamentary deputies. A law in 1928 decreed parliament to be no longer freely elected. Instead, the electorate voted for or against 400 candidates nominated by the Fascist Grand Council. In local government, elected municipal councils and mayors were replaced by nominated officials.

When it came to economic and social life it was the same situation of total, all-pervading fascist control. People had to join the fascist organisations, the *corporazioni*, if they wanted to keep their jobs. For children there was a fascist youth organisation, the *Balilla*. Even if they were not enthusiastic about the fascist state, most people could do little but accept it. It was difficult enough for anyone who was not a card-carrying fascist to get a job or be sure of continued employment. In addition to the *corporazioni* there was the Voluntary Militia for National Safety and a Special Tribunal for the Defence of the State, designed to eliminate political subversion with the help of its secret police, known as OVRA.

Mussolini's first aim was to make Italy strong internally and to achieve this he waged a number of social and economic "battles". The "Battle for Births" aimed at increasing Italy's population.

Women had to be driven back into the home, to be dutiful wives and mothers, and the more children they had the better. Mothers of seven children were given medals, pregnant women were saluted by militiamen, while unmarried men were liable to special, punitive taxes. Of course, Mussolini himself had to set a good example, so Rachele and the children were brought to Rome to live with him. But their family life was not as cosy as the propagandists made out. Even at home Mussolini spoke and postured as though he was presiding over a mass meeting while down-to-earth Rachele, honoured as the ultimate, stay-at-home fascist mother, called her husband *"Duce"*. As a father, Mussolini was closest to his eldest child, Edda, and he was pleased when she married a rising

Mussolini leads his officers "on the double". They were expected to jog into his office for their orders, and generally to set an example of ceaseless energy. Fascism was about action and fascists had to be permanently active.

young diplomat, Galeazzo Ciano.

Many other "battles" were waged. Extensive public works provided employment and boosted national morale. There were farm settlements for ex-servicemen and an ambitious scheme to reclaim the Pontine Marshes for agriculture. Less successful was the "Battle for Wheat", an attempt to make Italy self-sufficient in food production. This project was dear to Mussolini's heart, consistent with his image of a rural Italy brimming with children. He even wrote and published a poem about it. But fruit, oil and wine production were neglected at the expense of wheat crops which generally did not grow well where they were introduced.

But Mussolini at least looked as if he was doing something about Italy's problems and, as foreign observers noted, the fascists kept the trains running on time. Constant propaganda showed the *Duce*'s personal dedication. He was photographed everywhere – in magnificent uniforms, in his swimming trunks, stripped to the waist while he joined in with the harvest work. No one knew that the *Duce* needed spectacles for reading and that because of stomach ulcers he was on a strict diet. Instead, his personal fitness was made into a legend. Rather than walk down a line of troops, he inspected them at a jogging pace. To create an impression of superhuman energy the lights in his offices were left on long after he had gone home. And after all this hard work, the *Duce* allegedly found time for playing the violin, for reading Greek classics in Greek, for flying planes and riding horses, for fencing and playing tennis, as well as for chasing after every woman in sight!

THE CONCORDAT AND AFTER

In spite of his genuine hostility to religion, Mussolini was cautious in his relations with the Vatican, the seat of the Catholic Church. Because many Italians were sincere Catholics, he stood to benefit from a cordial relationship between the fascist state and the church.

Mussolini signs the Concordat in the Lateran Palace, 1929. Church and state had been at loggerheads in Italy since 1870, and for some time both sides had been keen to reach an agreement. However, after years of secret negotiations, it was the irreligious Mussolini who achieved the deal that was dear to the hearts of so many ordinary Italians.

Relations between church and state in Italy had been strained ever since the *Risorgimento*, when Papal territories had been seized to make up the Italian nation-state. To heal this old quarrel would be a considerable feat for any political leader. As a preliminary to the Concordat, the name for the series of treaties with the Pope which were eventually negotiated, Benito and Rachele Mussolini remarried according to Catholic rites. The Battle for Births was one of many fascist campaigns that appealed to the Church, as did the exemption of the clergy from taxation. Pope Pius XI, whose reign began in 1922, appreciated that Mussolini would be the best bulwark against godless socialism, and so the way was opened for a deal. By the Lateran Treaties of 1929 the Vatican was confirmed in its possession of the Holy See, an area the size of a large park containing the Basilica of St Peter's, the Piazza in front of it and the nearby Vatican buildings. Also, the Church was compensated for the loss of territory during the *Risorgimento* and Catholicism was recognised as the sole official religion of Italy.

The following years were the height of Mussolini's regime, in spite of the economic distress arising from the worldwide Great Depression of 1929. He continued his economic programmes in an atmosphere where open opposition was a thing of the past. By 1935 he felt secure enough to develop an aggressive foreign policy. Mussolini dreamed of an Italian empire as large as the ancient Roman Empire and he always called the Mediterranean *mare nostra* (our sea). As early as 1927 his troops had intervened to install King Zog as ruler of Albania, and as a result that country became a virtual colony of Italy. He backed every political movement that threatened the stability of Yugoslavia, as well as subsidising various anti-French and anti-British movements in Egypt and North Africa. He was jealous of those European countries which had substantial colonies and craved the same for Italy.

Ethiopia (Abyssinia) was to be the real beginning of this cherished empire. Although brown-eyed, dark-haired Italians were uncomfortable with Nazi celebrations of a blue-eyed and blond master race, by fascist definition Africans were definitely inferior beings and their colonisation was the "universal mission" of Rome. In 1935 Mussolini's forces invaded Ethiopia and after a

Italian soldiers, on their way to take part in the invasion of Ethiopia, display portraits of Mussolini on their troopship. International disapproval of this invasion, and of the atrocities carried out by the Italian forces, only served to heighten the *Duce*'s popularity at home.

very brutal campaign, which included the gassing of Ethiopian villages, he was able, in 1936, to give himself the new title "Founder of the Empire".

THE INVASION OF ETHIOPIA, 1935

During the early 1930s the Italians in Eritrea and Somaliland engineered various border disputes with neighbouring Ethiopia. One clash in 1934 led Mussolini to decide to invade Ethiopia. He gambled that France and other countries would not stop him. On 3 October 1935 the Italian Expeditionary Force invaded from Eritrea and within two days had captured various border towns. The Italians' advance was slow but by April 1936 Dessie and Gondar had fallen. On 14 April a second Italian force invaded from Somaliland and by 5 May the capital city, Addis Ababa, had fallen. The Italians won because of their superiority in weapons. Mussolini's gamble paid off in that neither Britain nor France took military action against his invasion.

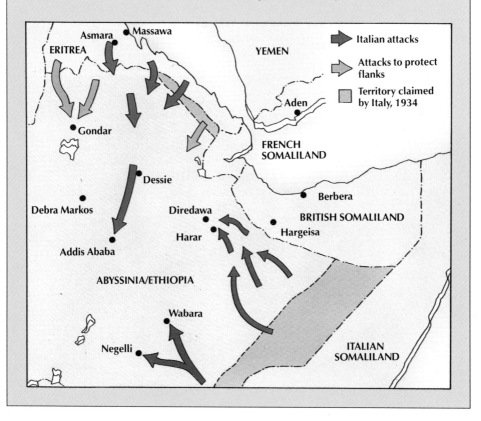

But the Ethiopian adventure outraged international opinion and in November 1935 the League of Nations imposed sanctions on Italy. Although Mussolini claimed delight at being hated by what he considered decadent and ineffectual foreign governments, and his popularity at home soared after the denunciations, Italy was isolated, with Nazi Germany as one of its few allies. There were many obvious and intentional similarities between Italian fascism and German Nazism. These were symbolised by Black Shirts and Brown Shirts, by *fasces* and swastikas. Although Hitler thought that some of Mussolini's antics – for example, the endless pictures of a bare-chested *Duce* – were quite ridiculous, he did admire the Italian leader and regarded him as an equal. It is even said that Mussolini was one of the few people that Hitler

Marshal Pietro Badoglio enters Addis Ababa, capital of Ethiopia, at the head of his invasion force. This conqueror's entry into the Ethiopian capital in 1936 would be reversed during World War II.

genuinely liked. For his part, Mussolini did not at first reciprocate this admiration and liking. He thought the German *Führer* was an effeminate upstart. Always sensitive about his short stature (some people said that the *Duce* recruited his aides on no other basis than the fact that they didn't make him look small), he resented Hitler's relative tallness and was put out when the German leader became internationally prominent as the major fascist leader.

Apart from these trivial issues, there were important reasons why Hitler and Mussolini were not immediate allies. They had serious differences about the future of Austria, Italy's neighbour as well as Germany's. Mussolini was close to the Austrian Chancellor, Engelbert Dollfuss, whose movement echoed Italian fascism more closely than it did German Nazism. Mussolini was very concerned when Dollfuss was murdered by Austrian Nazis in 1934. After that the prospect of a union between Germany and Austria (*Anschluss*) was only a matter of time, yet it was in Italy's interests that Austria should remain an independent buffer state.

After the invasion of Ethiopia Mussolini's doubts about Nazi Germany gradually changed to support. Although he criticized Hitler in private, in public he hailed the German leader as a "genius". Both Italy and Germany aided General Franco's Falangist rebels in the Spanish Civil War, which broke out in 1936, bringing the regimes closer together. Mussolini entered the war in the hope that he would gain military bases in the Mediterranean, but Italy's already over-stretched military resources became even more strained as a result of the country's participation. In fact the Spanish adventure had been far from glorious, and after a major defeat at Guadalajara, Franco hinted that he would be relieved if his amateur Italian allies went home. Needless to say, just as he had

Mussolini (middle) with the Austrian leader, Engelbert Dollfuss (in bowler hat on far left).

made sure that the Italian public didn't hear about military incompetence and atrocities in Ethiopia, this Spanish embarrassment was presented in the Italian press as a victory.

However, late in 1936 Mussolini was invited to Germany, where he was feted and flattered as a great world leader. No one was surprised by the ensuing friendship pact, the Rome-Berlin Axis. It was quite clear, in spite of propaganda to the contrary, that Hitler, who made a return visit to Italy in 1938, was the senior partner of this alliance. At home, Mussolini's deference to Hitler soon became irritatingly obvious. He personally inspected every inch of Hitler's route for his Italian visit and specifically Nazi influences were now added to fascist rituals: Italian soldiers had to adopt the goose step for their parades. More seriously, the *Duce* launched an anti-Semitic campaign in Italy. But this campaign, which was not followed up with the brutality of its German equivalent, was not popular. The Italian Jewish community was tolerated, if not respected, and even within Mussolini's regime Jewish individuals had been prominent. For example, his Finance Minister until 1935 was Jewish, as was his lover and first official biographer, Margherita Sarfatti.

Even the *Duce*'s most devoted followers now began to worry about his increasingly frenzied and irrational behaviour. From day to day, he would change his mind about foreign policy, sometimes motivated by trivialities such as an unflattering article about him in a French newspaper. Italian ambassadors abroad were never warned about what their head of government was about to say,

Mussolini with Hitler in September 1937. The *Duce* was never happy about the fact that the *Führer* was taller than him. Normally he took care to be photographed as a much larger man than he actually was.

and were left in the dark as to Mussolini's attitude towards world affairs. Their reports were unread and their letters were left unanswered. Even the Foreign Secretary, Mussolini's own son-in-law, Galeazzo Ciano, had no idea what might happen next. The *Duce* would boast to him that Italy possessed a secret war weapon but wouldn't say what this consisted of. At other times, to other people, Mussolini insisted that he had no intention of leading Italy into any major war.

Mussolini intervencd during the Munich Agreement of September 1938 in favour of a peaceful solution to Hitler's designs on Czechoslovak territory. In practice this "pacifying" role meant that he persuaded the other concerned powers – with the exception of Czechoslovakia, which was not represented – to let Hitler go ahead with his invasion. Then, when Hitler had annexed Austria and invaded the Czech Sudetenland, Mussolini decided to invade Albania, where King Zog was showing signs of resisting Italian influence. An Italian expeditionary force overran that country and in the following month, May 1939, the Axis pact was turned into a full-scale military alliance named the Pact of Steel (at first Mussolini, the incorrigible phrase-maker, had thought of calling it the "Pact of Blood"). Now Italy and Germany, in the event of being "involved in warlike complications with another power", had to come to one another's aid and "support it with all its military forces". Also, in spite of his earlier championship of China against Japan, Mussolini joined Germany and Japan in the Anti-Comintern Pact against communism (which meant the Soviet Union).

Mussolini was so used to talking his way out of awkward realities that he rarely considered the technicalities and strategies of war. But as the war he had been blustering about for years became imminent, Italy was without the right weapons or any real plan of operations. In signing the Pact of Steel, Mussolini trusted a German reassurance that there would be no major conflict for three years. In spite of his fantasies about Italy's might, he realised that the country was not ready to take a full part in another world war. The news of Hitler's Non-Aggression Pact with Stalin's Soviet Russia in August 1939 made nonsense of the Italian effort against communism in Spain, but the ever-adaptable *Duce* adjusted to this contradiction. After all, the combination of fascist Italy, Nazi Germany and Soviet Russia would be invincible. Even so, he tried to stall Germany's aggression. As Hitler prepared to invade Poland, Mussolini listed his country's immense requirements in arms and raw materials: coal, petrol, steel, machinery and ammunition. But Mussolini was not heeded. Hitler promised only some of these requirements and thanked the *Duce* for his help in non-military matters: "Even though our paths are now diverging, destiny will yet bind us to one another."

When World War II began in September 1939, Mussolini declared that Italy would not be a combatant, but when it looked as if Germany was about to have an early victory he had to enter the war. Otherwise, World War II would not result in the desired expanded Italian empire. On 10 June 1940, when France was on the verge of defeat, Mussolini declared war on Britain and France.

WAR AND DEFEAT

Mussolini's declaration of war on 10 June 1940 was met with more perplexity than enthusiasm among the majority of Italians, in spite of a torrent of propaganda to stir up support for the war. Apart from a general reluctance to enter a major war as Hitler's ally, there was a feeling that the *Duce* was not up to his self-appointed role as Italy's warlord.

Hitler and Mussolini at a meeting in Florence in 1940. In spite of all the smiles, by now the relationship between them was a fraught one, Hitler obviously having the upper hand. It did not help that Mussolini resented the help of interpreters even though his German was not very good.

It was getting harder for Mussolini to present himself as a superman. His age (he was now 56) and his various illnesses, especially the stomach ulcers from which he had been suffering for decades, were beginning to tell on him.

Although Mussolini had informed the king of his decision to enter the war, his close advisers and the Fascist Grand Council were not consulted. Moreover, in spite of the Pact of Steel, Mussolini refused to discuss a common strategy or joint long-term war aims with Hitler. Indeed the Germans were surprised, not to say disappointed, when the immediate Italian attacks on Malta, Egypt and Corsica, which they had been led to expect, did not happen. Instead, they heard about Italy's actual military initiatives, and these actions offered no reassurance. The troops which had been despatched to the French border by Mussolini had played a purely defensive and cautious role in France's defeat. It was only two days before the French signed the armistice of 22 June 1940 that Mussolini ordered his generals to make an offensive over the Alps.

As far as the *Duce* was concerned, the war would be finished when the French were finished. But before the war ended, he was hoping for a chance to fight the British, whose colonies in Africa he coveted. He tried to get Hitler to agree to a large Italian contingent in the planned invasion of Britain, and was annoyed when the Germans refused his help in this area. They insisted that they could handle Britain and that it would be far better, from the point of view of the Axis as a whole, if Italy concentrated on the Mediterranean theatre of war.

Hitler gradually assumed the role of supreme military commander of Germany's war machine. Although this ended disastrously, to a large extent Hitler earned his authority because he was seen to have been personally committed to the armoured warfare tactics that were so spectacularly successful in France. By contrast, Mussolini was supreme commander of Italy's armed forces from the very beginning of the war. Because fascism was so bound up with a glorification of war as a purifying bloodbath, its leader had to be naturally warlike. He could not be seen to be a mere politician, deferring to expert generals. But unlike the *Führer*, the *Duce* never did anything to inspire confidence in his authority as a military leader. Mussolini would announce sudden changes of plan to his generals, as though this were a sign of imaginative, fearless leadership. But his decisions were always made with an eye to superficial propaganda rather than a serious awareness of the complexities of the military situations into which he was sending his army.

After the fall of France, Mussolini's chief concern was that Italy should move fast enough to seize as much territory as possible before the German invasion of Britain brought the war to an end. Mussolini's eye fell on Greece and Yugoslavia. The *Duce* thought that the "liquidation" of Greece would be easy. To make his army seem larger he almost halved the size of Italian divisions, thus doubling their number, boasting then of the invincible numbers he had at his disposal. His army chief of staff, Marshal

Mounted Italian troops crossing a bridge on the Albanian-Greek frontier, as a prelude to the disastrous invasion of Greece.

Rodolfo Graziani, heard of the invasion of Greece after it had begun, when listening to the radio news. The chiefs of staff of the Italian Navy and Air Force had been told a few days earlier, but when they protested Mussolini simply ignored them: "If anyone makes difficulties about beating the Greeks I shall resign from being an Italian."

As a result, the Italian soldiers who set off to invade Greece did not know that there were no suitable ports for disembarking a large army on the far coast of the Adriatic. They were without adequate maps of the mountainous terrain they were about to penetrate and were not sufficiently aware of the hazards of the rainy season, which was about to begin. So blindly confident was Mussolini of a quick victory – an Italian *Blitzkrieg* ("lightning war") – that the troops were without clothing for temperatures below zero. The invasion was timed for 28 October 1940 but the Greeks were aware of it because Foreign Minister Ciano had been talking indiscreetly for days. Alarmed at the prospect of another disastrous Mussolini initiative, the Germans made enquiries, but the rumours of a Greek invasion were denied. Mussolini was afraid that his Axis allies would stop his attempt at a parallel war.

After the invasion, Hitler rushed to Italy to find out what was being planned. He brought his Chief of the High Command of the German Armed Forces, Field Marshal Wilhelm Keitel, with him, and was clearly interested in holding serious military talks. But the Italian equivalent, Marshal Pietro Badoglio, did not know about this conference until it was over. By then it was too late to halt Mussolini's blind rush for an easy and early victory all on his own initiative. Hitler tried hard to be diplomatic but was privately furious. He feared that such a badly planned campaign would damage the Axis in the eyes of states that were still officially neutral: Bulgaria, Turkey, Spain and Yugoslavia. Also, an Italian defeat might give the British a base for their planes in Greece. From this time on Hitler had little confidence in his Italian ally's military ability.

For the first few days bad weather kept Italian aircraft on the ground so that the Greeks were able to counter the invasion, pushing the Italians out of their country and into Albania within a month. For the next few months Mussolini had to fight a desperate and defensive war. Marshal Badoglio indiscreetly suggested that the campaign was being fought for ideological and propaganda reasons rather than military ones, and was forced to resign as Chief of the Armed Forces Staff. Although he had been exempted from income tax as a reward for his successes in the pre-war Italian invasion of Ethiopia, Badoglio had resented Mussolini since the early days of the March on Rome. Then, as a senior commander in the regular Italian Army, he had wanted to disperse the Black Shirts who were gathering so threateningly around Rome. Now, a scapegoat for the Greek disaster, Badoglio bided his time, waiting for the right moment to overthrow the *Duce*.

The *Duce*, far from the fighting, meets with Italian forces in Greece. He had hoped to take the Greek surrender in person, but no such opportunity would come his way.

In April 1941 the Germans attacked Greece and Yugoslavia and their campaign, which caused a postponement of the invasion of Russia, lasted three weeks. Mussolini maintained his armies on

THE FALL OF GREECE, 1941

By March 1941 the Italians were pushed out of Greece and had lost control of much of Albania. Hitler sent an army to help the Italians. The Greeks based their defence on holding a line from Xanthi to the border but their forces were too spread out. The German attack started on 6 April and quickly pushed through this line. In four days Thessaloniki was overrun. By 20 April the Germans reached Ioannina and Lamia. British troops were evacuated to Crete but on 20 May German paratroops landed there. The last British troops left Crete after ten days' fighting.

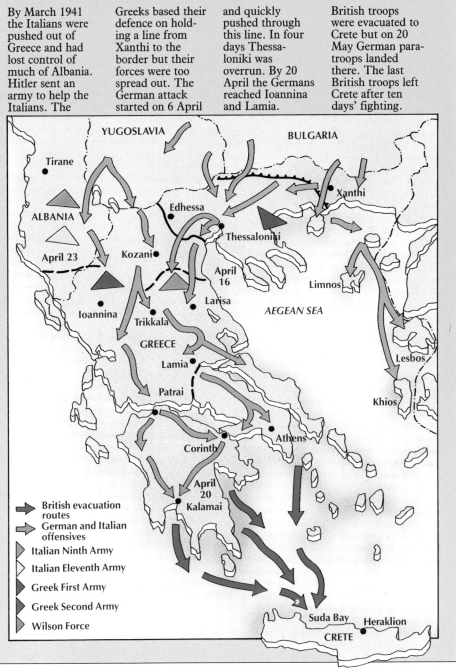

YUGOSLAVIA

BULGARIA

Tirane

ALBANIA

April 23

Edhessa

Xanthi

Thessaloniki

Kozani

April 16

Limnos

Ioannina

Larisa

AEGEAN SEA

Trikkala

GREECE

Lesbos

Lamia

Patrai

Khios

Corinth

Athens

April 20
Kalamai

➡ British evacuation routes
➡ German and Italian offensives
◢ Italian Ninth Army
◢ Italian Eleventh Army
◢ Greek First Army
◢ Greek Second Army
◢ Wilson Force

Suda Bay   Heraklion
CRETE

the defensive until the Greek resistance began to crumble. At the last moment Mussolini was hoping to go to Greece in time to take the surrender personally, but the Greeks obstructed this desire by surrendering to the Germans rather than the Italian Army. Half-sympathetic to the Greeks, Hitler thought about making peace with them, in return for an alliance. But Mussolini demanded a complete capitulation so that fascism could be seen to have triumphed. This disastrous Greek campaign left more than 100,000 men dead.

In North Africa Mussolini's troops fared no better. Because of his determination, against all the odds, that the Italians achieve a major victory in Africa on their own, Mussolini misled Hitler about the number of heavy tanks and other resources that were at his disposal. Before long, his forces in North Africa, lacking adequate air cover, had suffered a major defeat at the hands of the British Western Desert Force. It was at this stage, early in 1941, when the Italian campaign was in dire straits, that Mussolini had to appeal to Hitler for help. He responded by sending Major General Erwin Rommel and his forces to bail out the Italians. So as not to damage the *Duce*'s prestige, these German troops were officially under Italian command. More bad news came from East Africa. By May 1941 Ethiopia, "the pearl of the fascist regime", had been overrun by British and Allied troops. The Emperor Haile Selassie returned to his country and it regained its independence.

Within 12 months of the *Duce*'s declaration of war, the news from every battle front in which the Italians were active was devastating. But even though he alone was responsible for all important decisions, Mussolini never took the blame for defeat. Instead, he harangued his troops for being cowardly and unfascist, and his generals for being unworthy of such great leadership. All the while,

ROMMEL'S OFFENSIVE, 1941

On 12 February 1941 Major General Rommel arrived in North Africa to assist the Italian forces in Libya. Rommel soon realised that British forces in the area were weak. He decided to launch a lightning attack through Libya with only two divisions and push the British troops back into Egypt. He caught the British completely unawares. Rommel split his force into three, which confused the British, who evacuated Benghazi. In just over a month Rommel's troops were on the Egyptian border. The defeated British poured into the garrison town of Tobruk, which was now under siege. The siege would last more than six months.

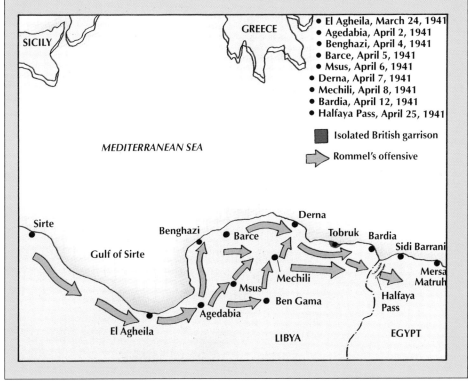

- El Agheila, March 24, 1941
- Agedabia, April 2, 1941
- Benghazi, April 4, 1941
- Barce, April 5, 1941
- Msus, April 6, 1941
- Derna, April 7, 1941
- Mechili, April 8, 1941
- Bardia, April 12, 1941
- Halfaya Pass, April 25, 1941

Isolated British garrison

Rommel's offensive

the obedient Italian press kept up a stream of morale-boosting lies. For example, it was frequently alleged that 12 million Italian soldiers were available for service, where in truth only a quarter of that number were ever called up. Again and again the Italian Navy, which lacked both radar and effective air support, was caught by the British Mediterranean fleet. In one three-minute engagement, during the Battle of Cape Matapan in March 1941, 2,400 Italian sailors lost their lives. Vainglorious lies, contradictory strategies and incompetence were costing lives. When an Italian naval commander boasted that he had sunk an Allied battleship, the other navy officials were sceptical because he refused to name it. But this fictional victory was good enough for the *Duce*. Against advice, he insisted on having the commander decorated.

Mussolini personally insisted on sending an Italian Army contingent to the German invasion of the Soviet Union, even though, once again, the Germans said that they would prefer it if the Italians concentrated on the Mediterranean and North Africa in particular. But the *Duce* was undaunted. The Italian soldiers who were sent to the Soviet Union were dressed in summer uniforms and wore cardboard shoes. They were pathetically ill-equipped for a Russian winter and by 1943 half of them had been killed or captured. Once again, propaganda rather than reality influenced Mussolini's decisions. Convinced that Germany was about to achieve an easy and early victory against the Soviet Union, he wanted the benefits of conspicuous Italian participation.

At this point in the war one Italian general estimated that 99 per cent of Italians had reached a point where they hoped Italy would lose the war. Many Italians who had put up with Mussolini because of their longings for a strong and stable government, but who were never at ease with the Axis alliance, were upset when America entered the war in December 1941 on the Allied side. The United States, to which so many Italians had emigrated and in whose armies so many Americans of Italian descent were serving, was a more natural ally of Italy's than Japan. At the same time Italy was suffering from serious food shortages and from British bombing. Italy was short of many of the raw materials it needed. It could only obtain oil from Germany, which was using all its supplies on the war effort.

In spite of the generally bleak outlook on the Mediterranean front, Italian naval forces scored a welcome victory without realising it. On 18-19 December 1941 three Italian midget submarines entered the harbour at Alexandria, in Egypt, under cover of dark. They knocked out two British battleships, the *Queen Elizabeth* and the *Valiant*.

In North Africa Rommel scored many victories and Axis troops were on the Egyptian border in June 1942. At this point Mussolini went to Africa with a large retinue of journalists and leading fascists, hoping to enter the Egyptian cities of Cairo and Alexandria in triumph. But his timing was wrong and his judgement mistaken. He stayed 500 miles (800 km) behind the front line – not a good position for a man who thought of himself as a valiant lion – and he was annoyed when

HUMAN TORPEDOES

The Italian Navy first started to develop "special attack" weapons in 1935. One of these was a manned torpedo, which was eventually built in 1940. They were officially known as SLC or *siluro a lenta corsa* (slow running torpedo) but they were known by their human operators as *Maiale* (Pig) because of the clumsy way they operated.

The Pig was 6.7 m long and had a nearly silent electric motor. Its crew wore rubber suits and had a supply of oxygen for six hours. The warhead was detachable and had a fuse which allowed five hours before exploding. From 1940-43 some 80 of these human torpedoes were built and tried out.

Spare breathing equipment and tool locker

The Pig could be submerged to about 30 m but only over a short distance. It travelled at 8.3 km/h.

The pilot of the human torpedo manoeuvred the craft with a steering-column which controlled the rudders.

Rudder

1.6 hp electric motor

Propeller

LEAVING
THE SUBMARINE

TRAVELLING UNDERWATER

Frogmen

Instruments and controls

On the night of 18-19 December 1941 three Pigs entered the harbour at Alexandria. They were able to set their warheads near the *Queen Elizabeth* and *Valiant*. All the frogmen were captured, but the ships were badly damaged.

300 kg (600 lb) explosive warhead

△ The *Valiant* before the war. The Italians did not realise that their men had damaged the *Valiant* and *Queen Elizabeth*.

Batteries

During the attack on Alexandria the frogmen ran into many problems. One Pig got its propeller stuck and one of the frogmen lost his breathing equipment. Nonetheless this was the most successful operation. Earlier missions had failed because of technical problems. The British responded to the attack by improving their harbour defences.

DEPOSITING WARHEAD WITH TIMER

MAKING GOOD ESCAPE

Rommel, whose popularity derived from his willingness to be on the front line, did not bother to meet him. After three weeks of feeling foolish, Mussolini had to return home, the newspapers lamely describing his visit as one of inspection.

The end of 1942 saw many setbacks for the Axis forces. In October-November 1942 Rommel's troops were defeated at El Alamein, Egypt, and Axis troops were forced out of Libya and started a long withdrawal to Tunisia. Also in November 1942 Allied troops landed in Morocco and Algeria and headed for Tunisia. Mussolini, ever-ready to blame his commanders, sacked Marshal Ugo Cavallero on 30 January 1943. He also dismissed his son-in-law, Ciano. He then asked for Rommel, who had made no secret of his low opinion of the *Duce*'s talents as a military strategist, to be dismissed, but Hitler refused this favour.

During these crises Mussolini was not an inspiring leader. In an increasingly unstable situation, it did nothing for the morale of his soldiers when he dismissed them as a "race of sheep". According to the *Duce* too many modern Italians were the descendants of the slave population of ancient Rome. That was why they were letting him down. He rapidly became thinner and older-looking, and at the same time his well-known affair with Clara Petacci did nothing to foster an image of the leader facing the same hardships as his people. His appearance on newsreels was received in stony silence. By the time British and American troops landed in Sicily on 10 July 1943, the majority of Italians welcomed them as liberators.

At this stage the *Duce* had to accept the fact that his military supplies were running short. Only seven infantry divisions, lacking in armoured cars, stood ready to defend Italy itself against the Allies. He had to arrange another difficult meeting with Hitler. Mussolini no longer looked forward to his encounters with the German leader. He made up for his feelings of inferiority with ludicrous gestures. Once, for example, when he was travelling in a German plane, he insisted on taking over the controls alongside Hitler's personal pilot, and demanded that this fact be recorded in the official communique arising from the subsequent meeting. Also, Mussolini refused to be accompanied by interpreters. Because his German was not in fact very good, this meant that he hardly knew what had been discussed and what had been agreed to, leaving his advisers, as well as the Italian Army and Navy commanders, in an impossible and embarrassing position.

The meeting took place at Feltre in Venetia, nine days after the Allied landing in Sicily. Mussolini was desperate for military aid, but the Germans were preoccupied with the fighting in the Soviet Union and could not spare the 2,000 aircraft requested by Italy. Instead of concrete help on his own terms, the *Duce* got a lecture from Hitler on his shortcomings. In future German aid would mean German control – in effect, German occupation of Italy. During this awkward and humiliating meeting Rome was being bombed by the Allies, and Mussolini was in constant pain from his stomach ulcer.

A few days later, on 24 July, the Fascist Grand

Council, Mussolini's hand-picked advisory committee, decided that the *Duce* was no longer fit to lead Italy out of its mess. He had to be removed while there was still time to negotiate a deal with the Allies. Summoned to meet them, Mussolini made a rambling, muddled speech. It was not good enough. The Minister for Justice, Count Dino Grandi, then proposed that the king and the parliament should re-assume their former powers, including the king's supreme command of the army, and take charge of the war. Marshal Badoglio, who was now 72 years old, would take over as prime minister. It amounted to a revolt against Mussolini's authority. Even his own newspaper endorsed it, taking Mussolini's name off the front page and replacing it with a photograph of the new leader Badoglio.

For the truth about what was happening to their country's participation in the war many Italians listened to British radio broadcasts. They were hoping to learn that peace had been declared as a result of the toppling of Mussolini. Instead they heard on the Italian news that for the time being the war would continue. Fearing, correctly, that as soon as it was apparent that he was trying to make a deal with the Allies the Germans would rush their forces southwards to hold Italy, Badoglio was playing for time. Thus began a period of uncertainty which became known as the "Badoglio 45 Days". However, the new government did immediately set about abolishing the main fascist organisations. A free press and an anti-fascist opposition began to re-emerge.

A bewildered and pitiful Mussolini immediately

began to compare his fate with that of Napoleon, and even with the betrayal of Christ. Rachele, who stuck with him in spite of all his infidelities, is rumoured to have teased him by saying: "You've had them all arrested, I suppose?", referring to his opponents. But on 25 July 1943 after a meeting with the king in which he was formally asked to resign, it was Mussolini himself who was arrested and placed under "protective custody".

First he was taken to the island of Ponza, off the coast between Rome and Naples, where his opponents in the past had languished. However, he did not remain there for long. Knowing that Hitler would not allow the *Duce* to remain a captive while he could still be useful, Badoglio had him moved to a small mountain hotel in the Abruzzi. But even this precaution did not work, for on 12 September 90 German commandos in 12 gliders effected a bold rescue operation. They carried "Karl-Heinz", the German code-name for Mussolini, off this rugged mountain to Vienna in a small plane, and

Mussolini arrives in Vienna after being rescued by German commandos in September 1943. The success of this bold rescue operation cheered him up, but not for long.

then to Munich, where he was met by his wife and family. Mussolini called his rescue the most romantic and bold escape operation in history.

The next day he went to Hitler's headquarters. Although the *Führer* welcomed him warmly, it was soon apparent that Mussolini was a broken man. He did not have the spirit to return to Italy to rally what survived of the fascist movement against the Allies, with whom, on 3 September 1943, Badoglio had at last arranged an armistice. Goebbels reported: "The *Duce* has not drawn the moral conclusions from Italy's catastrophe which the *Führer* expected." German troops were moving

Mussolini with Marshal Hermann Goering, soon after his rescue. He arrived at Hitler's headquarters to take part in discussions about future strategy. But already Mussolini looked like a broken man, and Hitler knew that he was only useful as a figurehead for a continuing fascist presence in Italy.

rapidly into northern Italy to forestall the Allied invasion. On 3 and 9 September Allied troops had landed in southern Italy and were making their way north. Hitler could not afford to let Mussolini retire. Not only did he need northern Italy's industrial resources – both the factories and the slave labour of the disbanded army – but Italy's natural mountain defences offered Germany precious time in the future battle for Europe. A puppet state had need of a puppet ruler. At the end of September, Mussolini was forced to set up a new fascist republic in northern Italy, which was occupied by the Germans.

This ill-fated republic became known as Salo, from the town where the Ministries of Foreign Affairs and Popular Culture were based. Mussolini himself was based in the small town of Gargnano on Lake Garda. After a few weeks of treatment by a German doctor – involving the elimination of milk, almost his staple food, from his diet – Mussolini became dramatically better, more his old self. It was with renewed vigour that he pursued this last-ditch stand for fascism. In January 1944, after a spectacular show trial, those members of the Fascist Grand Council who had not managed to escape the *Duce*'s wrath were executed. This gruesome scene was filmed. Mussolini had his own son-in-law and former foreign secretary, Galeazzo Ciano, executed. His daughter Edda managed to flee to Switzerland with her children, also keeping her husband's diaries and other papers, which were eventually published to give an intimate view of life around the *Duce* during his last years.

THE ALLIED INVASION OF ITALY

The Allies decided to make Italy their main objective for 1943. The operation in Sicily was successful and it was only a matter of time before Italy itself would be invaded. Meanwhile Mussolini was being ousted from power and the Allies invaded the mainland on 3 and 9 September, after the Italians had formally surrendered (on 3 September). Allied delays gave the Germans a chance to occupy Rome and improve their defences on the Gustav Line.

The Gustav Line held up the Allied advance for several months over winter. The Allies diverted their main effort to defeat Nazi Germany from Italy to France. They slowly worked their way up Italy. After the fall of Rome troops were withdrawn from Italy to invade southern France. The Allied advance was again halted for another winter on the Gothic Line. The Allies renewed their attacks on Italy in April 1945 and German forces there finally surrendered on 2 May.

◁ Allied troops land in Sicily. The landings here were quick and decisive, but the subsequent attack on mainland Italy was more arduous.

▷ With the help of Italian anti-fascist resistance, the Allies had to work their way up through the peninsula. This campaign saw some of the fiercest fighting of World War II.

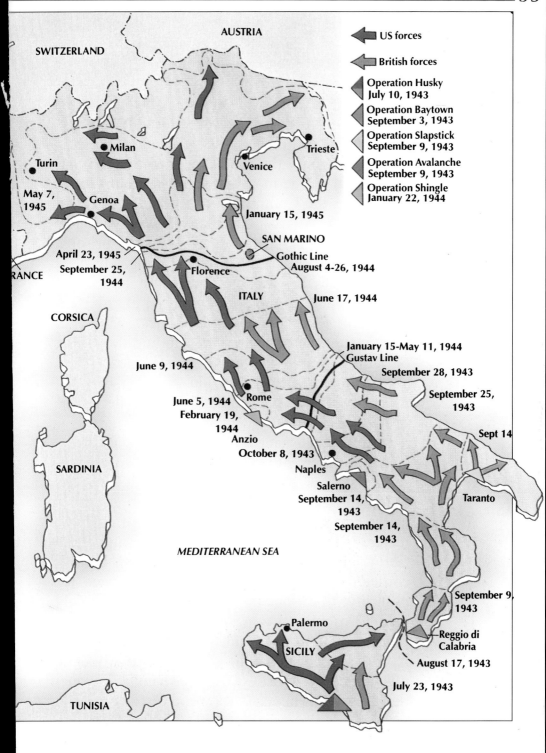

AUSTRIA

SWITZERLAND

US forces

British forces

Operation Husky
July 10, 1943

Operation Baytown
September 3, 1943

Operation Slapstick
September 9, 1943

Operation Avalanche
September 9, 1943

Operation Shingle
January 22, 1944

Milan

Trieste

Venice

Turin

May 7,
1945

Genoa

January 15, 1945

SAN MARINO

April 23, 1945

September 25,
1944

FRANCE

Gothic Line
August 4-26, 1944

Florence

ITALY

June 17, 1944

CORSICA

January 15-May 11, 1944
Gustav Line

June 9, 1944

September 28, 1943

September 25,
1943

Rome

June 5, 1944

February 19,
1944

Anzio

October 8, 1943

Sept 14

SARDINIA

Naples

Salerno

September 14,
1943

September 14,
1943

Taranto

MEDITERRANEAN SEA

September 9,
1943

Palermo

Reggio di
Calabria

SICILY

August 17, 1943

July 23, 1943

TUNISIA

Northern and southern Italy were now under different rule and were separated by a fighting front. But whereas in the south anti-fascist political groupings had emerged and were being encouraged by the Allies to take over local administration, in the north, where the Germans and fascists were still strong, the resistance was underground and military. The most active resistance organisations were the Communist Party and the Action Party. Their partisan bands, swelled by prisoners of war who had escaped from fascist prisons, harried the Germans. As the fighting advanced northwards, the war became more and more savage. Whole communities suffered ghastly reprisals for their resistance activities. Mussolini sanctioned many atrocities – including the killing of ten partisans for every fascist killed – and allowed fascist gangsters to do whatever they felt necessary. His own violent end would reflect these brutal decisions.

Within what remained of the fascist state the Germans were totally dominant. Mussolini's republic was a colony of the Third Reich. This was humiliatingly obvious. When Italian factories closed down because of a shortage of war materials, the plant was summarily shipped to Germany. In his final months Mussolini became conscious of a need to tidy up his image for posterity. In the 600 days that Salo existed he only held 17 cabinet meetings, behaving more like an eccentric philosopher than an iron-willed dictator. Ever the propagandist, he now had to show that he was as much a victim of the Germans as anyone, that it was not his fault Italy and fascism were in ruins. But even his newspaper memoirs were censored by the Germans. He visited Hitler at his Wolf's Lair headquarters in East Prussia just after Count Claus von Stauffenberg's unsuccessful assassination attempt of 20 July 1944. Apparently, it consoled him to see the *Führer* himself becoming equally vulnerable.

By the spring of 1945 the Allied armies were pushing the Germans out of northern Italy and Mussolini began to prepare for a historic last stand. It was important that he should leave Italy in style and with a large retinue. But this was not possible. As the partisans drove the Germans from the cities of Milan, Turin and Genoa, Mussolini heard that the Germans were about to surrender unconditionally without even consulting him. With a few remaining followers, including his mistress of the previous eight years, Clara Petacci, he tried to escape to Switzerland. But at Dongo, far up Lake Como's western shore, he was captured by the 52nd Garibaldi Brigade of partisans and shot. Clara Petacci pleaded to be killed with him. On the following morning, 29 April, their bodies were taken back to Milan and strung up by the heels. It was a grim end to the *Duce*'s career. Some 24 hours later Hitler committed suicide.

Afterword
At the time of his death Benito Mussolini was the most hated man in Italy. Behind him lay a country destroyed by military defeat and civil war. Fascism had made the trains run on time, but in the long run it was a disaster for Italy. In the general election of 1946, when women voted for the first

time, the great majority of votes went to three large parties: the Christian Democrats, the Socialists and the Communists. By a referendum the people decided in favour of a republic rather than a monarchy. Victor Emmanuel, who was compromised by his collusion with Mussolini, had abdicated in May 1946. He was succeeded by the crown prince, Umberto, who left Italy after the elections to retire in Portugal.

The postwar treaty required Italy, in spite of its renunciation of fascism and its practical contribution to the latter part of the war against Germany, to surrender a considerable part of its fleet and to reduce the numbers of its army, air force and navy. On the economic side, reparations had to be paid to Russia, Yugoslavia, Greece, Ethiopia (Abyssinia) and Albania. The African colonies, Libya, Eritrea, Ethiopia and Italian Somaliland, had to be given up. The other Allies renounced their claim on reparations, recognising, in Churchill's words, that Italy had "worked her passage home" by contributing to Germany's defeat.

It was 1957 before Mussolini's body, in a rough coffin, was handed over to Rachele Mussolini for burial in the cemetery at Predappio, where he was born. Black Shirts give the fascist salute as the coffin lies in the cemetery chapel.

In practical terms Italy was recognised as a victim rather than an active agent of World War II. Sympathy was deemed more appropriate than punishment. By the time a provisional government took power in 1947, the United Nations Relief and Rehabilitation Administration (UNRRA) had poured into Italy more than $418 million worth of supplies and services. Then the new Italian government financed additional programmes of relief. At the price of war and terrible devastation, a modern Italian democracy survived the legacy of Mussolini and fascism.

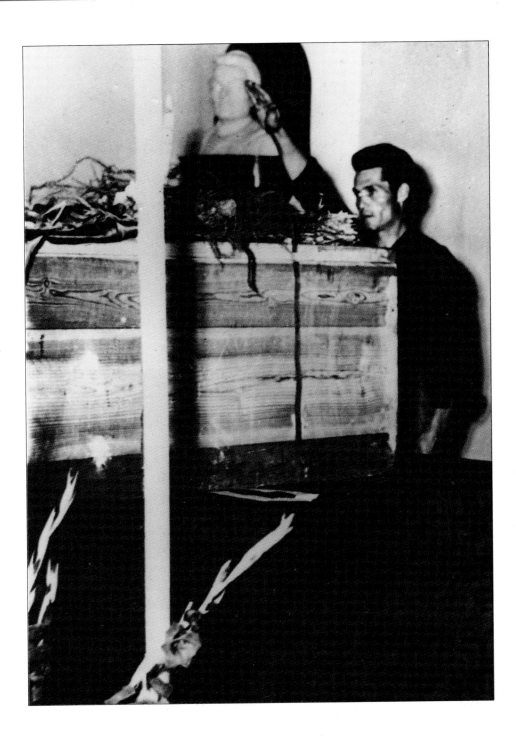

CHRONOLOGY

1883 29 July, Mussolini is born.

1902 Mussolini qualifies as a primary teacher and leaves Italy to spend some years in Switzerland working at odd jobs and as a political activist.

1909 Mussolini works on a socialist newspaper in Trento.

1910 Benito and Rachele Mussolini set up house together.

1911 Mussolini is arrested and imprisoned for protesting against the Libyan war. He becomes editor of *Avanti!*.

1914 Mussolini starts his own newspaper, *Il Popolo d'Italia*.

1915 Mussolini serves as a soldier in World War I.

1917 After being wounded, he returns to the home front.

1919 D'Annunzio leads a raid on Fiume. The *Fasci di Combattimento* are founded and are soon organised into a political party.

1921 The fascists win seats in parliament.

1922 Mussolini becomes prime minister of Italy after the October "March on Rome".

1923 By the Acerbo Law, which changes the electoral rules, the Fascist Party gains control of parliament.

1924 After the election of 1924 a leading opposition politician, Giacomo Matteotti, is murdered by Mussolini's followers.

1927 Mussolini backs King Zog in Albania, making a virtual Italian colony of that country.

1928 The Italian parliament is abolished.

1929 By the Lateran Treaties a Concordat, or agreement, is made between the Italian state and the Catholic Church.

1934 Chancellor Dollfuss of Austria, an ally and friend of Mussolini, is murdered by Austrian Nazis.

1935 Italy invades Ethiopia (Abyssinia) and is condemned by the League of Nations.

1936 Italy intervenes in the Spanish Civil War as an ally of Franco. The Axis Pact is signed between Italy and Germany.

1937 Italy joins the anti-Comintern (anti-communist) pact between Japan and Germany.

1938 Mussolini supports Hitler's objectives during the Munich Agreement (negotiations over the Czech crisis).

1939 May, the Axis Pact becomes a full-scale military alliance, the "Pact of Steel"; September, German invasion of Poland begins World War II.

1940 June, Italy declares war on France and Britain; September, Italian forces invade Libya from Egypt; October, Italy invades Greece; December, British troops begin driving the Italians from Egypt.

1941 February, Italians defeated at Beda Fomm in Libya; March, Italy attacks Greece from Albania, the British enter Ethiopia (Abyssinia) and Rommel begins his first offensive in Libya; April, Germany invades Yugoslavia (surrenders 17 April) and Greece (surrenders 21 April); May, Emperor Haile Selassie re-enters Ethiopia; June, Hitler invades Soviet Union. December, the Japanese attack on Pearl Harbor brings the United States into World War II.

1942 July, first battle of El Alamein in Egypt; October, second battle of El Alamein; November, Allied landings in North Africa.

1943 May, final surrender of Axis forces in Tunisia; July, Allied landings in Sicily. Mussolini is arrested and replaced by Marshal Badoglio; September, Italy makes peace with the Allies. After being rescued by German commandos Mussolini is installed as head of the Salo Republic; October, Italy declares war on Germany.

1944 January, Allied landings at Anzio in Italy; May, Monte Cassino is captured by the Allies; June, Rome is liberated.

1945 April, final Allied offensive in Italy is launched. As he attempts to flee Italy for Switzerland Mussolini is captured by partisans and executed. Next day German forces sign an armistice in Italy. Hitler commits suicide; May, Germany surrenders; August, atomic bombs dropped on Hiroshima and then Nagasaki. Japan surrenders.

GLOSSARY

Allies the big countries that fought against Germany, Italy and Japan during World War II – Great Britain, France, the United States, the Soviet Union and China.

anti-Semitism hostility to Jewish people. It has its origins in religious intolerance and economic jealousy.

Axis, the Rome-Berlin the name given to the co-operation of Mussolini's Italy and Hitler's Germany between 1936 and 1945. The word "Axis" was first used by Mussolini in a speech in 1936. Later the countries which fought the Allies in World War II were known as the Axis Powers – Germany, Italy, Japan and later Romania, Bulgaria, Slovakia and Hungary.

communism the belief that all property, including land and industry, should be owned by the community rather than by individuals.

Concordat the word for a series of treaties, the Lateran Treaties, by which the Catholic Church and the Italian state were reconciled in 1929.

corporazioni the organisations set up so that all Italians, including children, would join the fascist movement.

Duce literally means "leader". Mussolini's preferred title.

fascis literally means "a bundle" and refers to the bundle of sticks carried by the *lictors* who marched in front of officials of the Roman Empire. Because of these ancient imperial associations, *fascio*, from which the word "fascist" derives, was not an unusual term for radical political groups in Italy.

Irredentism the nationalist belief that Italy's frontiers should be pushed forward to include all Italian-speaking peoples living in the regions that were still part of the Austro-Hungarian empire.

manganello a bludgeon or club used as a weapon by fascists.

Munich Agreement a deal in September 1938 between the leaders of Britain, France and Italy (and excluding Czechoslovakia) which allowed Hitler's Germany to break up Czechoslovakia in return for promising not to occupy the non-German regions of that country.

nationalism the belief that individual communities or cultures – usually defined by a common language – should be independent and self-determining, rather than part of an empire.

partisan a guerrilla fighter of the anti-fascist resistance in European states, such as France, Italy and Yugoslavia. They were often members of the socialist and communist opposition to fascism.

propaganda information designed, by distortion if necessary, to win people over to a certain version of events.

Salo the name by which Mussolini's last government became known. This fascist republic was in effect a German puppet state, with its Ministries of Foreign Affairs and Popular Culture based on the small town of that name.

socialism the belief that income and wealth needs to be distributed fairly.

syndicalism a revolutionary movement to secure political control by workers through direct trade union action.

FURTHER READING

Ciano, Edda Mussolini *My Truth* (A Zarea Ed.), London 1976

Collier, R *Duce! The Rise and Fall of Benito Mussolini*, London 1971

Deakin, F W D *The Brutal Friendship: Mussolini, Hitler and the Fall of Fascism*, London 1962

Grindrod, M *Italy*, Ernest Benn, London 1968

Hibbert, Christopher *Benito Mussolini: A Biography*, Longmans 1962

Mack Smith, D *Mussolini*, Weidenfeld & Nicolson, London 1981

Thomson, D *Europe Since Napoleon*, Penguin 1974

Wiskemann, E *Europe of the Dictators 1919-1945*, Collins 1966

INDEX

Photographic Credits:
Cover and pages 4, 7, 15, 18, 25 and 28: Popperfoto; pages 12, 20, 23, 27, 32, 36, 38, 47, 48, 53 and 57: Topham Picture Library; page 34: Hulton Picture Company.